AT THE POND

Taylor Farley

CRABTREE
PUBLISHING COMPANY
WWW.CRABTREEBOOKS.COM

At the pond . . .

I wear boots.

I use a net.

I catch a fish.

I find a frog.

I see a turtle.

I feed the ducks.

I have a picnic
with my friends.

We all help to keep it clean.

I have fun at the pond.

Glossary

boots (boots): Boots are a type of footwear. They cover the feet and part of the legs. They usually keep water out to help feet stay warm and dry.

catch (kach): To catch is to capture or take hold of something that is moving.

net (net): A net is made of pieces of material woven together. It is used to catch animals and insects.

picnic (PIK-nik): A picnic is a meal eaten outside.

Index

boots 4
cleanup 18
ducks 14
fish 8

frog 10
net 6
picnic 16
turtle 12

School-to-Home Support for Caregivers and Teachers

Crabtree Seedlings books help children grow by letting them practice reading. Here are a few guiding questions to help the reader with building his or her comprehension skills. Possible answers are included.

Before Reading

- What do I think this book is about? I think this book is about a pond. It might tell us what children like to do when they visit ponds.

- What do I want to learn about this topic? I want to learn which animals live in ponds.

During Reading

- I wonder why... I wonder why the boy wears boots at the pond.

- What have I learned so far? I have learned that fish, frogs, turtles, and ducks live in ponds.

After Reading

- What details did I learn about this topic? I learned that people work together to help keep the pond clean. They pick up garbage.

- Read the book again and look for the vocabulary words. I see the word **_catch_** on page 8 and the word **_picnic_** on page 16. The other vocabulary words are found on pages 22 and 23.

Library and Archives Canada Cataloging-in-Publication Data

Title: At the pond / by Taylor Farley.
Names: Farley, Taylor, author.
Description: Series statement: In my community | "A Crabtree seedlings book". | Includes index.
Identifiers: Canadiana 2020038807X |
  ISBN 9781427129536 (hardcover) |
  ISBN 9781427129635 (softcover)
Subjects: LCSH: Ponds—Juvenile literature.
Classification: LCC QH541.5.P63 F37 2021 | DDC j577.63/6—dc23

Library of Congress Cataloging-in-Publication Data

Names: Farley, Taylor, author.
Title: At the pond / by Taylor Farley.
Description: New York, NY : Crabtree Publishing, [2021] |
Series: In my community : a Crabtree seedlings book
Identifiers: LCCN 2020050770 |
  ISBN 9781427129536 (hardcover) |
  ISBN 9781427129635 (paperback)
Subjects: LCSH: Pond ecology--Juvenile literature. |
Ponds--Juvenile literature.
Classification: LCC QH541.5.P63 F37 2021 | DDC 577.63/6--dc23
LC record available at https://lccn.loc.gov/2020050770

Crabtree Publishing Company

www.crabtreebooks.com   1-800-387-7650
e-book ISBN 978-1-947632-67-7
Print book version produced jointly with Crabtree Publishing Company NY, USA

Written by Taylor Farley
Production coordinator and Prepress technician: Amy Salter
Print coordinator: Katherine Berti

Printed in the U.S.A./012021/CG20201112

Content produced and published by Blue Door Publishing LLC dba Blue Door Education, Melbourne Beach FL USA. Copyright Blue Door Publishing LLC. All rights reserved. No part of this book may be reproduced or utilized in any form or by any means, electronic or mechanical including photocopying, recording, or by any information storage and retrieval system without permission in writing from the publisher.

Photo Credits: cover and page 5 © Shutterstock.com /Cultura Motion; cover illustration of frog © Shutterstock.com/ languste; page 3 © Shutterstock.com /tbmnk; page 7 © Shutterstock.com /Phovoir; page 9 © Shutterstock.com /Sergey Gerashchenko; page 15 istock.com/ MNStudio; page 11 © Shutterstock.com /Svetlana Foote; page 13 © Shutterstock.com /spetenfia; page 17 © Shutterstock.com /Tomsickova Tatyana; page 17 © Shutterstock.com /Matt Jeppson; page 19 ©istock.com/ monkeybusinessimages; page 21 ©istock.com/ Stock Photos | Lifestyles; page 23 ©shutterstock.com/ FamVeld.

Published in Canada	Published in the United States	Published in the United Kingdom	Published in Australia
Crabtree Publishing	Crabtree Publishing	Crabtree Publishing	Crabtree Publishing
616 Welland Ave.	347 Fifth Ave	Maritime House	Unit 3 – 5
St. Catharines, ON	Suite 1402-145	Basin Road North, Hove	Currumbin Court
L2M 5V6	New York, NY 10016	BN41 1WR	Capalaba QLD 4157